Contents

CW01558847

MILLENNIAL MONEY MANAGEMENT
Chapter 1 – Intro

A few years ago, a friend of mine came to me and asked if I would sign up to a night school class with him. He'd watched Grand Designs a bit too much and wanted to build his own house, but subsequently realised how little he knew about DIY and how much contractors charge. He pointed out to me how much of my pay cheque seemed to go to workmen (who I relied upon to fix everything in my rickety old house) and how maybe it was high time we learned a bit ourselves. He may have also wanted someone to drive him to the huge warehouse like building on the edge of town where we showed up for 3-hours between six and nine every Tuesday night. I was sceptical at first; my only experience with a saw came from secondary school woodworking class and I hadn't exactly been a natural – I'm pretty sure the balsa wood clock I made for my Mum accidentally found its way to the bin. However, it turns out learning as an adult who can see the value in a certain set of skills and wants to learn is sometimes a lot easier than learning as a child. For ten weeks we measured, cut, and drilled. We soldered together pipes, smeared a bit of plaster and even practiced laying a few bricks. Steve built the house (I put in a good few shifts cutting and putting up plasterboard) and while I still call the occasional workman out I feel I have a better-than-average idea of what he's doing (and I haven't needed anyone to put a shelf up for me recently).

The key thing is that a little bit of education can go a long way. I know right now it's more popular to scream and shout (at the TV or the phone screen) about how the world is broken and pretty much going to hell, but I prefer to look at what an amazing time we live in. So much information is just there, walking around with us in our pockets waiting to get out. With a basic understanding of what you are trying to achieve, and a vague idea of the direction you might head in to get there, we have the collective genius of hundreds of thousands of experts open to us and incredibly cheap to consume. My mission with this book is to help you develop that primary, basic understanding, because when I headed out to my DIY course at least I had Year 9 Woodworking to fall back on – for many of us economics, finance and investment were not even on the curriculum.

I started looking after people's money 10 years ago, and one trend I've seen unfold during my career has me slightly worried. I've started to see the sheer amount of people who cannot afford to pay someone like me and my team to give them the help and advice they need to manage their wealth.

When I started out it was possible to walk into our office with about £50,000 in your account that you wanted to invest, and we would go about helping you. But the years that have gone by have seen more and more regulation fall upon private wealth managers. I saw first-hand the real cost of the crisis, and the years of austerity that succeeded it, so I have no intention of leading the charge for lower regulation – I think it's right that the people who look after other's savings are held accountable when things go belly up – but it has increased the cost of looking after each individual client many fold. As a direct result, the company I now work for will not consider you as a client unless you have at least £250,000 to invest – five times the amount (I'm not going to name names in this book but a number of our competitors don't want to look at anything less than £500,000). These are amounts of money that are out of reach for a vast majority of people, particularly in their earlier years of saving, and as a result the **advice gap** is opening its jaws wider.

The problem as I see it is that without access to advice you are going to have two options.

Option 1: The Ostrich Solution: stick your head firmly in the sand and refuse to take it out again regardless of what problems may start occurring around you.

Option 2: The DIY Solution: start learning a bit for yourself. Take an interest in how some of this fits together so that you can make a few informed decisions for yourself. I am not saying that you need to drop everything and enrol for a Masters in Finance, just that with a little understanding you are going to stand a much better chance of hitting your financial goals than the Ostriches.

You've made it far enough to read this, so I assume you picked Option 2.

In this book my mission is to provide enough information for you to make better decisions about your savings and investments. I realise that not everyone is like me (that's a nice way of saying I know I'm a bit weird), and that this subject can be a tad on the dry side. That's why I've aimed to keep the chapters to a comfortably short length and why (with the help of a good friend of mine) we've included a lot of pictures and diagrams to liven things up.

So why should I care?

I understand that there may be a few of you who are still considering being an ostrich, but you've decided to give me to the end of Chapter 1 to convince you to stay. And for that I've got a few good answers, but the best one by far is that you need to;

Reason One: Beware the Inflation Monster.

So, we all know someone like him, he's not an entirely bad guy but if you let him get out of control, he's going to drink ten beers and ruin your birthday party. Inflation is a natural phenomenon in a consumer society – as the whole economy grows, we create more wealth, we create more babies, we ask for pay rises, we buy more stuff, the babies grow up, they ask for pay rises etc etc. As the level of **demand** rises the **prices** of things also rise. If you want to see a real world example of the havoc wrought by inflation go to the shop and see how many Freddo's you can buy for 10 pence.

Generally inflation is ok, our earnings tend to rise alongside prices so we can still afford to pay our rent, take care of the bills, run our car, and have a little left over at the end of the month for a ridiculously expensive Freddo. You might even be able to squirrel some cash away and build a savings account, but this is one area where inflation can turn particularly nasty. If you are stashing some cash for your future you want to be sure that when the future comes around you can at least buy the same amount of stuff with it – in fact, since you deprived yourself of that stuff in the past you want a reward for not having spent it. You don't want your savings lying around doing nothing, you want your savings to be down at the gym getting buff – your savings have a monster to fight.

If your savings are invested well the returns you can generate should be able to outgrow inflation. This is particularly true when you can take a really long-term view since you will begin to benefit from the effects of **compounding returns**.

Let's say for the sake of argument that I invest £1,000, and I can reasonably expect a 5% return on my money in an average year. Assuming I get that return I'm left with my £1,000 plus my £50 interest.

$$£1,000 * 105\% = £1,050$$

Now, I could at this point pat myself on the back, take my £50 interest out as cash and find the nearest barman to give my money to. However, assuming I don't desperately need any of this cash I can leave it all where it is and go for another year.

$$£1,050 * 105\% = £1,102.50$$

Not only do I get the £50 interest on my initial £1,000 but I get an extra £2.50 on the returns I made in the first year. In order to extend the formula out to multiple years and cover any potential investment amount and rate of return we do the following:

Investment Amount * (100%+ expected % return) to the power of the number of years you invest

Continuing our example, what if I were to happily leave my £1,000 compounding at 5% for 30 years;

$$£1,000 * 105\%30 = £4,321.94$$

These numbers start to look a lot more appealing. Now let's just say I can consistently put away £1,000 every year for those 30 years and get my 5% average return. I fell back on Excel a bit;

Year	Starting Balance	Interest	End Balance
1	£1 000	£50,00	£1 050,00
2	£2 050,00	£102,50	£2 152,50
3	£3 152,50	£157,63	£3 310,13
4	£4 310,13	£215,51	£4 525,63
5	£5 525,63	£276,28	£5 801,91
6	£6 801,91	£340,10	£7 142,01
7	£8 142,01	£407,10	£8 549,11
8	£9 549,11	£477,46	£10 026,56
9	£11 026,56	£551,33	£11 577,89
10	£12 577,89	£628,89	£13 206,79
11	£14 206,79	£710,34	£14 917,13
12	£15 917,13	£795,86	£16 712,98
13	£17 712,98	£885,65	£18 598,53
14	£19 598,63	£979,93	£20 578,56
15	£21 578,56	£1 078,93	£22 657,49
16	£23 657,49	£1 182,87	£24 840,37
17	£25 840,37	£1 292,02	£27 132,38
18	£28 132,38	£1 406,62	£29 539,00
19	£30 539,00	£1 526,95	£32 065,95
20	£33 065,95	£1 653,30	£34 719,25
21	£35 719,25	£1 785,96	£37 505,21
22	£38 505,21	£1 925,26	£40 430,48
23	£41 430,48	£2 071,52	£43 502,00
24	£44 502,00	£2 225,10	£46 727,10
25	£47 727,10	£2 386,35	£50 113,45
26	£51 113,45	£2 555,67	£53 669,13
27	£54 669,13	£2 733,46	£57 402,58
28	£58 402,58	£2 920,13	£61 322,71
29	£62 322,71	£3 116,14	£65 438,85
30	£66 438,85	£3 321,94	£69 760,79

If I kept that up, I would be sat on **£69,760.79** at the end of those 30 years.

So, as long as we keep building and compounding our savings at a rate higher than inflation, we're much more likely to retain the **purchasing power** of our money and keep the inflation monster at bay.

Reason 2: We're living longer and we're having fewer babies.

Very few people really like talking about getting old and dying. This is something we need to get better at. Data from an ONS study in 2018 showed that by 2068 there are likely top be an additional 8.6 million people aged 65 years and over – a population roughly the size of London.

According to the latest mortality rates, a man like me born in the UK in 1987, is expected to last until 2067. With advances being made in modern medicine these figures are likely to be underestimating the true numbers for a lot of us. While this is awesome in so many ways, it is going to mean that we are going to need to stretch our savings further. Working longer is one answer to this, but most of us wouldn't want to push this too far;

Besides, my parents are happily retired, and they make it look like a lot of fun.

On the other hand we are slowing down on the baby making In 1947 there were 20.5 births per 1,000 people in the UK – in 2017 this had fallen to 11.1. Leaving aside the funny side of statistics that has you wondering how you get 0.1 of a baby, this has some implications for us all.

Historically, as people get older there were enough working age people to support them in their retirement. We all pay our taxes and this goes towards the State Pension. If our demographics continue to change as they have been, it will be dangerous to rely purely on the Government for your retirement.

Reason 3: You need to take your seat at the table.

We live in interesting times, and I am sure that when they get around to writing history books about the early 3rd Millenium they will make good reading. In many ways the planet seems to be at a crossroads – at the time of writing Greta Thunberg graces the cover of Time magazine as their person of the year, while a climate change denier sits in the White House.

We live in a capitalist democracy, I know that some readers will be less thrilled than others by the capitalist part of that – but this is it, it's the one we've got and it's unlikely to change without something radical happening. But elections and referendums are not the only time that you can vote to change the world you live in.

Companies have a huge impact on our planet, our society and our lives. They do harm – they pollute the environment, they exploit some of the poorest people out there, they make it easy to opt-in but hard to opt-out, they make people buy shit they don't need, and they often don't even pay their taxes.

But it is often also companies that do some of the best things in the world. They connect us to each other regardless of distance, they develop new technologies, they cure diseases. It will almost certainly be a company that cures cancer and a company that will put the first person on Mars.

I'm not trying to push my ethics on to you. I'm not interested in telling you what you should believe in or what you should think is ok and not ok. But I want you to know that how you invest your money is a way in which you can express your own personal morals. Investors own companies. The bosses report to you, they run the company for you and it's only by getting your seat at the table that you can affect the change you want to see.

Last chance to be an ostrich.

Your House is not your wealth –
IT'S YOUR HOME

When you're thinking about investment you need to build an overall picture of your personal finances. For many of us our first goal is to get ourselves up on the property ladder and if you have home-owning, baby-boomer parents it will almost certainly be something they encourage. I know some of you will be reading this from the comfort of your own castle.

I certainly don't want to sound like I am dissuading you from home ownership. I think buying a place to live has a huge number of benefits – both financial and non-financial. But the one thing I would discourage is ever considering your house or flat to be part of your true wealth.

People often say they are saving for a rainy day, so stop and take a minute to consider what one looks like. Maybe your car just got wrecked when you misjudged driving through a flood on the way home from work (true story, not my proudest moment) and you're going to need £3,500 to fix it or buy a new one. Or, maybe your little brother has just confessed that he missed his last four rent cheques and he needs a couple of thousand to clear his debts and keep his possessions off the street.

Ask yourself in these sorts of situations would you sell your home? Most likely you're riding your rusty 11-year-old push bike to work, and your little brother is still asleep on your futon.

Realistically, it will take an awful lot to make you sell up. You may do it to move up the ladder to your next property, or if you want to move to a new city. Maybe when you're older and your kids have flown off to nests of their own you will be able to downsize to a cheaper property and take some of your money out of the property market. But, for little emergencies or to meet smaller goals, most of us are not going to view our house as a backup bank account.

Some people would describe themselves as asset rich but cash poor. This is particularly true when a large portion of your personal finances are tied up in your home. When thinking about your investable wealth only really think about your cash. Think about the money that you could get your hands on reasonably quickly.

MILLENNIAL MONEY MANAGEMENT
Chapter 2 – Economics 101

Before we really get into it it's impossible to really talk about investments and financial markets without first thinking about The Economy.

In order to invest money well we need to try to understand where we are now and predict where we are going. Economics is going to help us with this. Just to warn you, I know that when you assume you make an ass out of u and me, but in economics we're going to have to assume a lot.

Key Assumptions in Economics

1. **Cost & Benefit:** economists believe that everything must have a cost and a benefit, and that people weigh up the two when they make decisions. You decided to read this book; I hope there will be some benefits for you, but there is an associated cost. Your time. The cost is all the other things you could be doing instead – you could be training to become a mini golf champion, earning a bit of spare cash moonlighting as an Uber driver, or (lets face it) binge watching the latest shows on Netflix. Economists refer to this as opportunity cost You have made the decision to read this book, so hopefully you weighed up the costs and decided that the benefits outweighed them.

2. Scarcity: this goes hand in hand with cost & benefit. Scarcity is the assumption that we do not have infinite resources. Your time is limited by the hours in the day so you were forced to decide how to spend it. It would not be possible to be a crazy golfing, Uber driving, Netflix watching, better informed investor. This is probably for the best.

In the wider world, scarcity exists in terms of all types of resources. We don't have an infinite supply of labour or raw materials so we have to have a way to decide who gets what and what we do with it.

3. The Law of Supply & Demand: governs the relationship between buyers and sellers and the price they agree upon.

Markets exist for practically every conceivable thing on earth. A market is simply any place two parties come together to exchange goods.

Let's say I have 2 tickets for a gig that I would l like to sell (I forgot Mum's birthday) and that you would like to buy (you forgot your Mum's birthday and it's her favourite band). Supply is equal to demand and we're going to find a price we're both happy with. It's a win win.

But now let's say both you and your sister forgot Mum's birthday and you both want to take her. There are still only 2 tickets, but demand is outweighing supply – there is a **shortage** of tickets. Suddenly I sense an opportunity to profit from your sibling rivalry and the price is going up!

However, my friend Adam overheard us talking. He's got a whole bunch of tickets available for the same gig and he swoops in, flooding the market. There is now a surplus. Supply is outweighing demand and I'm dropping my price to make a sale.

The price at which supply and demand meet is called **equilibrium**.

Types of Economic System

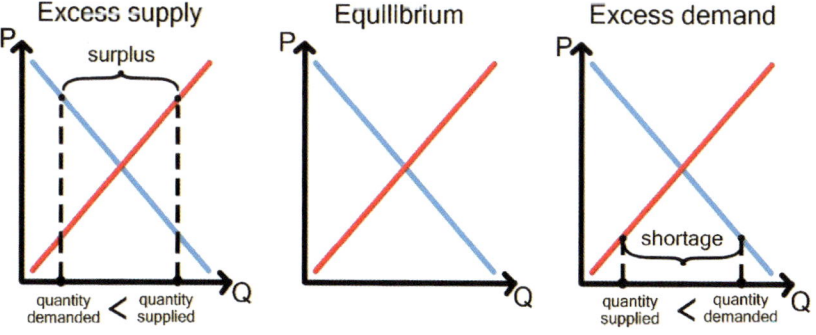

Free Market Economies & Planned Economies

Let's look at two extreme types of economic systems, that exist at opposite ends of the scale.

Planned Economies: alternatively the government can really stick it's oar in and take central control of the economy.In his book Das Kapital Karl Marx argued put forward the key **Factors of Production: Land, Labour and Capital.** Under a **Planned** or **Command Economy** the government controls all of these and decides how they are used and shared amongst people. While this might sound a lot like Communism, Communism actually takes things a step further – getting rid of the idea of **Private Property** and instead sharing everything equally amongst people. In this way, in theory, the idea of social classes would be destroyed.

Free Market Economies: involve little to no interference from the Government and are the most extreme form of **Capitalism**. Politicians take a **laissez-faire** approach; staying out of the way and letting businesses and households look after themselves. Individuals own **Private Property** and companies control **the Means of Production** (factories, offices etc). Adam Smith coined the phrase invisible hand in his book The Wealth of Nations. Free Marketeers believe that if left to their own devices, **supply** and **demand** will drive one another until prices reach **equilibrium** and the economy will essentially run itself in an efficient way.

In the real world neither of these systems truly exist. North Korea is probably the closest example of a Command Economy that exists in the world today – but even there reports and research has shown that informal markets exist as does an element of private property. On the surface The People's Republic of China is a Communist nation, but really it is a market economy with a high level of **Socialism**.

Meanwhile, countries such as Singapore and New Zealand operate very light levels of government and regulation but we need governments to provide certain things. Governments are responsible for key areas like;

Maintaining the rule of law by hiring police and judges and making sure there are courts.

Spending on defence to protect the country from attack.

Arranging welfare for people who have fallen on hard times.

Governments can also provide additional services for people depending on how much they want to get involved. For example in the UK our government provide us all with universal healthcare through the NHS, but in the USA far less healthcare assistance is provided and most people pay for private insurance.

Most economies are **mixed economies** with an element of free markets, but also some level of involvement by the government. **The Circular Flow Model;** is a great way to see how **Households, Firms and Governments** interact.

Households (people like us) want to buy goods and services from **Firms** (companies that produce things). We buy these for cash in the **Product Market**. But, in order to get some cash so that we can buy the stuff we want we need to sell something. Households primarily sell **labour** to Firms in return for cash in the **Resource Market**.

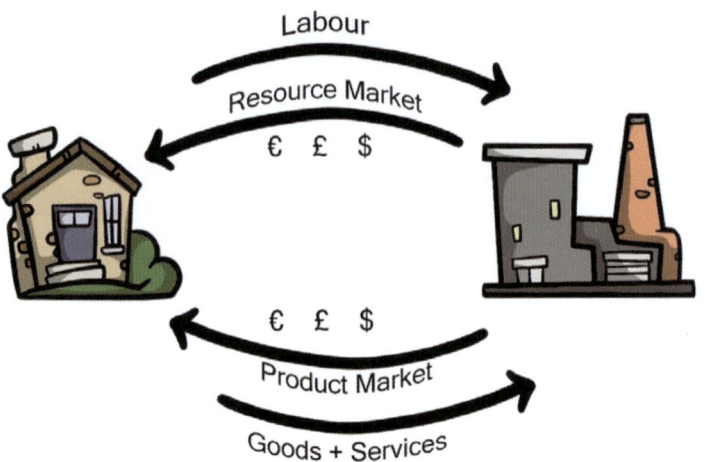

Governments take provide services to both **Households** and **Firms**, raising money from both in the form of **taxes** to pay for them.

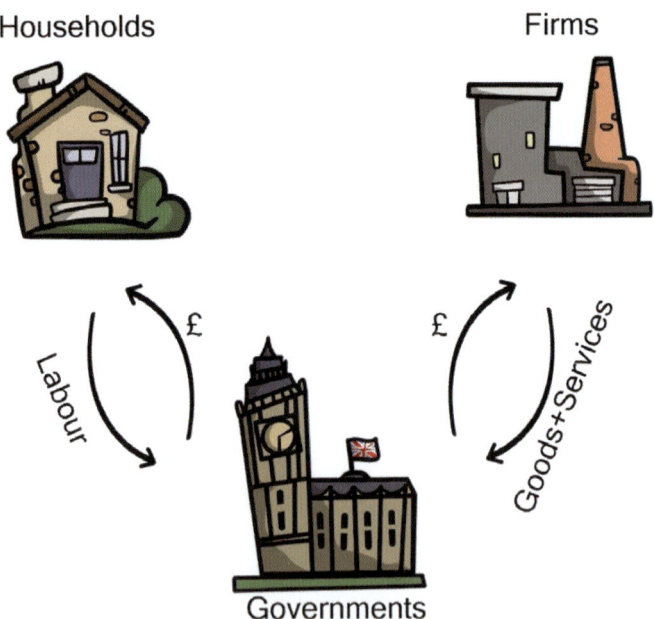

Governments also participate in the Resource Market – paying households for labour (firefighters, police, civil servants etc), and buy goods and services from **Firms** in the Product Market (computers, cars.

This all fits together in the **circular flow model**.

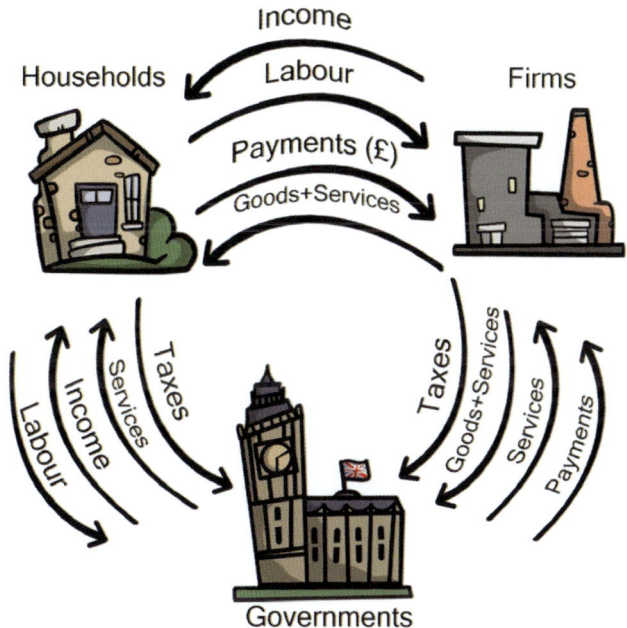

The Cycle

Economists and investors like to talk a lot about **the cycle**. This describes how the economy moves between periods of growth (or **expansion**) and contraction (or **recession**). The high points of continued growth are known as **peaks**, while the low point of a recession is known as a **trough**.

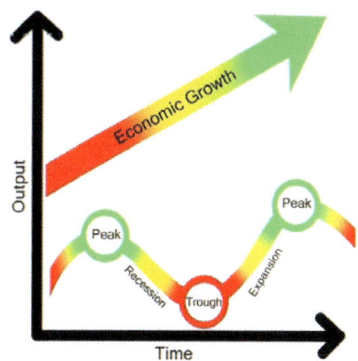

When economists talk about recessions they mean a period of six months where the economy has shrunk in size. The term **depression** is used to describe a particularly long recession. Meanwhile a long, large expansion is called a **boom**.

Bulls & Bears: economists and investors spend a lot of time arguing about whether the economy is on its way up or down. We call those who think things are on the way up **Bulls**, and those who argue we're heading downwards are **Bears**. The names are thought to originate from how the animals attack – **Bulls** thrust their horns up, while **Bears** swipe down.

Governments can get involved to try and control, or smooth the cycle using different types of **policy**.

Fiscal Policy: describes government spending. Economist John Maynard Keynes put forward a theory that governments should decrease their spending during periods of expansion – allowing businesses to take the lead; hiring workers and providing services. But, increase it during recessions to pick up the slack and avoid high levels of unemployment.

Monetary Policy: is the realm of Central Banks (like the Bank of England in the UK or the Federal Reserve in the US). The primary tool of Central Banks are **Interest Rates**. If the economy is struggling and cooling down, they cut interest rates, encouraging households and firms to borrow and invest more, giving the economy a boost. However, if the economy is running too hot and is in risk of burning up, they raise interest rates, making it less appealing to borrow money.

In a lot of developed countries, the Central Bank operates independently from the Government. In the UK for instance the Chancellor appoints the Governor of the Bank of England, but then allows him or her to get on with setting Monetary Policy. The Government can set the Central Bank targets (the UK government want the BoE to keep inflation at around 2% per year) but generally stay out of the way.

The Government maintains full control over Fiscal Policy. This is largely outlined in **Budgets** announced by the Chancellor.

Indicators

Much like the indicators on a car, economic indicators show where we are and our direction of travel. **Lagging Indicators** look back at data, while **Leading Indicators** look forward and try to predict what is coming. When we look backwards we get a much clearer picture since our indicators are based on things that have actually happened, but while lagging indicators are more accurate they only tell us where we have been and can be less useful at spotting what is coming next. Imagine you're driving down a motorway, in the rearview mirror it's a clear, Summer's day – but when you look out of the windscreen it's a blizzard.

Lagging	VS	Leading
Gross Domestic Product (GDP): is a broad measurement of the overall size and value of the economy. It tracks the value of all goods and services produced within a country over a period (most often a year).	Measure the size and growth rate of the economy.	A Purchasing Managers' Index (PMI) is made up of survey data asking supply chain managers in a range of industries about how confident they are feeling and how they intend to invest money in the coming year.
Retail Sales: show the volume of sales in stores up and down the country – giving a picture of how much people are spending.	Measure the strength of consumers	Consumer Confidence: is measured with a series of surveys asking thousands of households about their financial situation and how they expect things to change in the near future.
In the UK the Retail Price Index (RPI) and Consumer Price Index (CPI) both track basketsof commonly bought items. They measure how much prices go up or down each month. Economists also keep an eye on Wage Growth to see how much people are getting paid as more money in the system can drive inflation upwards.	Measure Inflation	Inflation Expectations Surveys: monitor the views of households and firms, and how they think inflation will change over the coming months and years.
The Unemployment Rate keeps track of how many people who are actively seeking jobs are unable to find them.	Measure Employment	Economists can track vacancies to judge how many jobs are out there waiting to be filled by employers. The Purchasing Managers Index also includes a section on hiring intentions.

(Some of the) problems with surveys:

While there is a fantastic amount of data out there in the world we do have to take some of it with a pinch of salt. Surveys are, by their nature, tricky things to get right – all sorts of biases can kick in that skew the results. Furthermore, some of the data is less reliable than the rest. Governments are often responsible for gathering and releasing data from their country, in some instances this leads to some questionable official figures. In a paper published in 2019 by the Brookings Institute economists estimated that the Chinese economy is about 12% smaller than official figures indicate.

MILLENNIAL MONEY MANAGEMENT

Chapter 3 – Taking Risk

Risk is not bad. Not understanding the risk you are taking is bad

Risk has a bad rep. We are taught through most of our childhoods to avoid taking risks, but to start with we need to take a fresh look at risk. The goal here is to become a rational risk taker.

You see, when your mum inevitably asked you something along the lines of...

...I would argue that she failed to give you enough information.

Maybe you could have asked her some follow up question.

And then there are questions you should ask yourself.

Let's imagine your Mum has provided you with some more adequate information and you've asked yourself a few questions, so you can finally understand why Jimmy's so keen on jumping off cliffs.

I can swim!
I'm reasonably good
of jumping.

The cliff is 8 metres high, mildly scary but not terrifying.

There is a rock that you have a 10% chance of hitting.

There is a fine loot at the bottom left by scurvy seadogs.

Let's try to not to be too morbid. You're not going to die if you hit the rock – you're just going to lose all the money you have in your pocket when you jump.

This should help you make an informed decision on whether to jump or not.

We should always think about **risk** alongside **return**. We shouldn't be willing to take risks just for the thrill of it. That's gambling. But in this scenario, you're not jumping off the cliff because you like the feel of the wind in your hair – the potential return is the pirate treasure.

There are a lot of different types of risks to consider when investing, but the first and foremost one that we're looking at here is the risk of **permanent loss of capital**. If you hit that rock, the cash in your pocket is going to float away into the ocean and make a lucky little crab very happy.

Investment is all about taking calculated risks and demanding returns that compensate you for them. That's the only way to generate the kind of returns you are going to need to defeat the inflation monster and hit all your financial goals.

Before you start investing it is worth asking yourself one key question.

How much can I afford to lose before it changes my standard of living?

I know it seems like a strange question at first – we're probably looking to make money not lose it. But, it's important to be aware of how much you can afford to lose before you would have to make changes to the way you live your life – if you lose a certain amount would you stop going on holiday? Or would you have to sell your car? Or maybe have to move somewhere cheaper?
Understanding this about yourself will help inform your decisions about how much of your overall wealth you can afford to invest in longer-term, riskier investments, and how much you should keep in safer, but lower return, cash accounts.

Diversification

At this point people usually start talking about eggs and baskets, but I was born in a city in the late 80's and eggs have always come in neat cartons from a supermarket for me. Instead I like to think about it in terms of extra lives.

What if rather than jumping off the cliff once with all your pocket money in your jeans you could have multiple tries. You must take some of your cash with you each time, and the treasure chest has less gold in it.

Assuming you jump more than 10 times, you are probably going to hit the rock on one of your jumps. But you stand a decent chance of getting the treasure on a number of your attempts This then has the potential to make up for the occasions where you lost your money.

Investors build **Portfolios** to help moderate the risks they are taking. A golden rule is to avoid sticking all of your money in to one investment – by diversifying the investments that you hold you can greatly reduce the overall level of risk that you are taking.

MILLENNIAL MONEY MANAGEMENT
Chapter 4 – Asset Classes & Portfolios

Now we've covered a bit about economics, risk and return it's time to start thinking about investing. In this chapter we'll look at some of the key **asset classes** and begin to consider putting them together to build a **portfolio**.

Asset Classes: are a group of investments that share certain characteristics. The major asset classes are **Cash, Equities** and **Bonds**. But we'll also look at some minor asset classes, including; **Property, Infrastructure & Renewables,** and **Commodities**.

Major Asset Classes

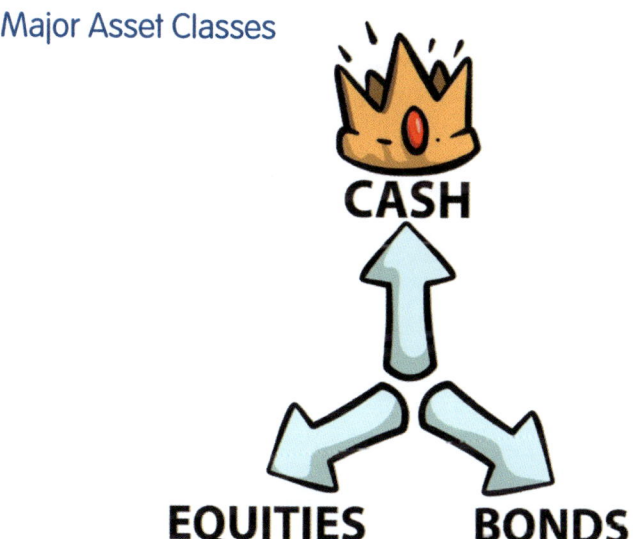

Cash is King. While it is one of the least exciting investment opportunities in the world, cash is by far one of the safest. If you need money in a hurry for an emergency, your cash investments should be your first port of call – therefore it's always important to have a healthy cash reserve before you consider riskier investments. However, this relative safety and ease of access comes at the price of low return (and the inflation monster is always waiting in the wings).

I don't know why but in finance there are often a few different names for the same thing! Equities are also known as Shares or Stocks. Bonds can also be called Fixed Interest or Fixed Income.

When thinking about the differences between **Fixed Income** and **Equities** I like to imagine a friend starting his or her own business. Let's say your friend Jamie comes to you one day and says he's tired of the humdrum world of Formula 1 race car driving.

What he's always dreamed about is running his own artisan coffee shop and bakery.....for cats.

It's probably in Shoreditch.

The only problem is that he somehow doesn't have enough money left over from his F1 days, and he needs £5,000 to get things off the ground. We're rational risk takers by now, so let's assume that the Cat Café actually has a solid business plan behind it, Jamie's a capable, honest set of hands, and this is an amount of money that you could help him with, without putting yourself in any financial difficulties. You've got a couple of choices about how you invest your money though.

On the one hand, you could lend Jamie the money. He'll need some time to get the café up and running but since he can start turning his coffee and cake into cash pretty quickly, he should be able to pay you back. While you wait for your money back, he can also afford to pay you some interest on the loan. Before you lend him the money, you're going to want to agree some terms (and probably write them down in a contract). How much are you giving him? When does he have to pay it back? How much Interest is he going to pay you and when is he going to pay it? This is effectively a Fixed Income investment.

The good thing (for you) is that regardless of how well business is going Jamie's going to have to pay you. You rank high on his list of priorities and so stand a better chance of getting paid; if a business doesn't pay its debts on time then it can collapse and be declared bankrupt. However, if Jamie turns out to have spotted a brilliant niche in the market and makes an absolute fortune out of his business, he is only ever going to have to pay you your £5,000 and your interest. You don't ever get paid any more than what was originally agreed (hence the fixed part of fixed income).

On the other hand, you could offer to become his partner. You could make an investment in his business in return for a share of it – or **equity** in the company. In doing so you would become a **shareholder** in the business.

If the business struggles to make ends meet, then you are in the trenches with Jamie. If there's no money in the till then there's no money in your pocket, and unlike with the loan there's no point at which Jamie is required to give you your money back. He will need to pay all his bills and any debts before he considers paying you anything, and if the worst comes to the worst and the business folds then you would probably stand to lose all your investment.

However, as the business starts to turn a profit, he can pay shareholders a bit of income in the form of a dividend – a share of the profits from the business – based on the percentage that you own. If Shoreditch turns out to be just the start for this budding entrepreneur and he builds a huge, cat café empire your money will continue to grow as the business grows and if he were to ever sell the company your shares would get bought out at the same time (more on that later). There is technically no limit to the amount of return that you can make as an equity owner, but the risks are notably higher.

As a shareholder in the Cat Café you also get a say in how the business is run through **voting rights**. If Jamie wants to make a big change, like bringing on board more investors or deciding to pay himself a fat bonus cheque, it may be subject to a shareholders vote – at which point you would be able to say whether you agree or disagree with his strategy. If enough shareholders object to the idea then management will have to come up with a new idea.

Similarly, investors can put their cash to work buying equities and bonds. These are listed on **stock exchanges** allowing everyone to keep track of the current prices they can be bought and sold for. Stock Exchanges, like the London Stock Exchange (LSE) or the New York Stock Exchange (NYSE) also help to match buyers and sellers, allowing all kinds of investors to get their money in and out of investments. Investors value different **securities** (any tradable financial instrument) based on the potential risks and expected future returns.

Equities	VS	Bonds
A financial instrument that carries an **ownership interest** in a company	What is it?	A financial instrument representing a **debt** that the issuer has agreed to pay back with interest
Companies	Issued by	**Companies and Governments**
Dividends: management decide how much to pay out of profits. The company cannot pay dividends if it cannot afford its debts	Income	**Interest:** the issuer must pay the agreed interest payments or risk going bust
There is no limit on potential upside if the company does well	Potential Returns	Return is limited to the agreed interest payments and repayment of the debt
100%: if a company goes bust the value of the company's equity tends to fall to zero	Potential Losses	100%: if the issuer defaults the value of the debt can fall to zero. However, the issuer will take all measures it can to avoid this and bondholders may be able to get some money back through **administration**
Equity holders get **voting rights** allowing them to have a say in how the company is run	Benefits	Holders get preferential treatment when it comes to getting repaid.

Defaults

Businesses or governments can **default**. This is where they don't have enough cash in the bank to either repay their debts or make interest payments. However, just because a business has gone bust does not mean there is no value left in it. One of my most striking memories from the Financial Crisis was when Woolworths went belly up (the Pick & Mix there was a particular loss to society in my opinion). After Woolworths went bust in December 2008 the stores continued to open as usual for weeks afterwards. **Liquidators** take control of failed businesses and **wind them up** on behalf of banks and bond investors who are owed money. They will do everything they can to squeeze the final pennies out of a business – at Woolworths I remember walking around and seeing price tags on the shelving units. Every asset of the business that can be sold is sold and investors get paid depending on where they rank in the **capital structure**. Banks and creditors – those who have provided goods and services to the company – get their money back first. Then if there's any money left after the banks are paid in full bond holders can be paid back. Finally, if (and this is a very big if) there is any money left then equity investors can get paid.

Priorities

1. Banks and Suppliers

2. Bondholders

3. Shareholders

Minor Asset Classes

Alongside the major asset classes of **Cash, Equities** and **Bonds** there are a number of other smaller investments that can be added to portfolios. These can be particularly useful for increasing diversification since they don't necessarily behave in the same way.

Property or **Real Estate:** investors can make money through owning buildings and renting them out. We tend to avoid **residential property** (houses and flats for people to live in) and instead focus on **Commercial Property** – offices, warehouses, and factories – since when companies lease these, they tend to do so over much longer periods of time.

Infrastructure and Renewables: we often think about bridges, hospitals and schools being built by the government. But to save money the government often arranges for these infrastructure projects to be funded using money from investors. Companies build the project and the government then either rents it off them (in the case of a Hospital or School) or allows the company to charge people for using it (hence the £5.60 charge to cross the Severn Bridge into Wales). In more recent years investors have backed a number of Renewable Energy projects in the same way – raising funds to build wind farms and solar panel arrays. They put the money up front but are rewarded over the long-term as the projects generate electricity that is sold into the grid.

Commodities: it is possible to buy physical commodities like precious metals, oil and grains. **Commodities** can be split into two major categories: **Hard Commodities** are things like Gold and Oil where the commodity does not have a shelf life and can stay in your possession indefinitely. Meanwhile, many agricultural products like wheat and soybeans would be considered **Soft Commodities**. It is possible to gain access to **commodities** through the shares of companies that produce them (you could buy shares in a company like BP to get exposure to **oil**) but to make it a true alternative to equities you could buy a physical barrel of oil.

Historically, financial instruments linked to commodities were designed to help producers plan for the future. A farmer, deciding what crops to plant in her fields is placed in a bit of a risky position.

She knows what the prices of wheat, corn, maize and soybeans are now, but the crops will take time to grow and in that time prices can change. She'll also have to invest money in to producing the crop before she can harvest and sell it; machinery, labour and fertiliser will cost the farm money. There's no guarantee that when she comes to sell the return, she will get will have covered her costs (let alone leave her with a profit).

Futures Contracts allow her to lock in a price for her crops – they are simply an agreement between a buyer and a seller to trade commodities for cash at a certain price on a certain date in the future. When you use instruments like **Futures** to cover yourself in this way you are **hedging** (think of hedging your bets). The farmer is then free to worry about the actual business of farming, as opposed to spending all her time trying to work out which way the prices of certain commodities are going.

Investors can also buy **Futures** if they expect the prices of commodities to go up, but if it is done in isolation then this is called **speculating**. Unlike in most of the other asset classes that we have looked at there is no **income** or **earnings** from a barrel of oil or a bar of gold. Investors are relying instead on supply and demand for the commodity to change in their favour.

Asset Allocation

Most modern wealth managers will recommend that investors build a **Multi-Asset Portfolio**. Different asset classes carry different levels of risk and behave differently depending on the overall economic climate.

At a simple level – bonds tend to offer lower returns but are less risky, while equities tend to be riskier but offer the potential for higher returns.

By combining different asset classes together, we can build a **diversified** portfolio. The following chart shows the returns over the last twenty years from a portfolio made up just of Equities, a portfolio made up just of Bonds, and a portfolio made up of 50% of each.

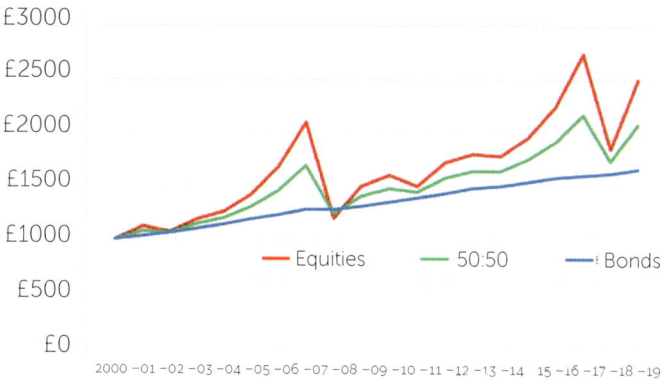

Some people might look at the red line and ask why not just invest in equities? After all in this example you come out with a higher return in the end. However, the trade-off is in the risk that we're taking – you might not be comfortable with the sharp downwards movements you saw in certain years (like 2008). Meanwhile, the portfolio of just Bonds might provide you with a lot less sleepless nights but not generate the kinds of returns you are looking for. The blended portfolio achieves a better return, but the **drawdowns** you suffer in certain years are not as severe.

Because they can move in different ways it is theoretically possible to build portfolios from multiple assets that are less risky than any portfolio of just one type. Investors talk a lot about **Correlation**. When assets are **Positively Correlated**, we expect them to generally move in the same direction, whereas when assets are **Negatively Correlated** we expect them to move in opposite directions given certain market conditions. Assets which are **Uncorrelated** are much like teenage children – they don't care what anyone else is doing they just do their own thing!

By combining different asset classes, we can build portfolios that are potentially less risky than one made up of any single type of investment. When they build portfolios a lot of investors are searching for the **Efficient Frontier**. The point at which you can get the best level of return for a certain level of risk by combining different assets.

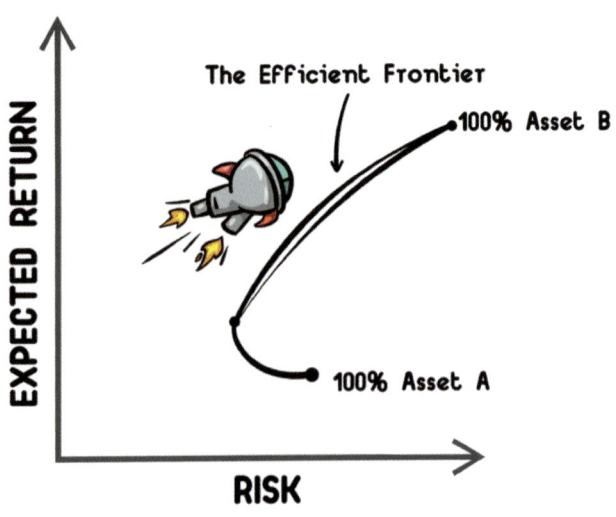

MILLENNIAL MONEY MANAGEMENT
Chapter 5 – Asset Selection and Valuation

Once you've decided how much of your portfolio you want to allocate to different asset classes you need to start thinking more about which investments you want to buy and how much you are willing to pay for them. This process is called **Asset Selection**. Assuming you have watched a film like Wolf of Wall Street at some point you've probably heard something along the lines of.

However, if it was quite that simple, I'd be sat on my own tropical island as opposed to writing this book, hiding away from a 'mild' Scottish winter.

Valuation is the way in which **analysts** and **investors** try to determine what exactly low and high are, in order to decide whether they are paying a good price for an investment. It involves looking at the key risks of an investment, the potential rewards and comparing similar investments with one another.

Analysts: job roles in investment companies can be quite specialised. Personally, I am more of a generalist – I look after clients, consider potential investments and build portfolios. However, we rely on **Analysts** to provide detailed views on potential investments. They're a bit like Wizards locked away in their towers – gazing into their crystal balls. Don't worry, we let them out for long walks.

Types of Investment Risk

Remember when I said there were a lot of types of risk? It's true that the **permanent loss of capital** is the key one we need to worry about. However, there are a number of more specific risks that investors worry about when they are deciding a fair price for a particular investment. The five risks outlined below are a few of the most notable.

Stock-specific Risk: this is the risk of a company or government getting into trouble that affects the value of investments in it but does not have an impact on the wider market. A good example of this is the Macondo Disaster in 2010. The Deepwater Horizon oil platform suffered a catastrophic failure resulting in a terrible environmental disaster. Investors immediately moved to reprice BP's shares – reflecting that it would lose all revenue from drilling in the Gulf, and would likely have to pay out huge fines and the costs of cleaning up the spill. **Stock-Specific Risk** is the key reason we **Diversify** our holdings.

Market Risk: Regardless of how well your portfolio is **diversified** it will be exposed to global events that can affect the whole of the market. Economic events (such as recessions) and Geo-political events (such as wars) can send the whole of the market down as a new price is found for investments that reflects the new world order. At the height of tensions between North Korea and the USA in 2019, stock markets reacted to price in the potential threat of war between the two countries. Admittedly, the markets did not see this as a particularly likely outcome; otherwise, everybody would have been too busy stockpiling canned foods and hiding under tables. But the fear was enough to send equities down lower while bonds rose as investors sought out safer assets.

Interest Rate Risk: is a type of **Market Risk** that particularly effects **Bondholders** but applies to other investments to a lesser extent. If you've been paying close attention (which I'm sure you have) you'll remember that back when we talked about economics, I mentioned that Central Banks adjust **Interest Rates** to encourage / discourage people to borrow money. A side effect of this is that the prices of bonds go up and down in the opposite direction. If interest rates rise then investors will require more interest to lend to companies and governments, therefore the price of existing bonds will go down to reflect this. As a Millennial it's sometimes hard to imagine a period of high interest rates. Since 2009 rates have been extraordinarily low in the wake of the Financial Crisis, with the Bank of England not rising rates above 1%. However, my Dad has mentioned from time to time the difficulty of paying a mortgage in the 1980's when the BoE base rate was rarely below 10%.

Default Risk: this is the key one when it comes to **permanent loss of capital**. Defaults often spell the end of the road for companies and; while investors may be able to recover some of their money through **administration**, it is far from guaranteed that they will see a single penny

Inflation Risk: That pesky monster is always out there waiting to sink his teeth into our savings. Inflation is a big issue for investors, and if we see it growing we demand higher returns so that we can defeat it. Therefore, if inflation grows investors expect to pay less for investments so that the expected returns stand a better chance of outpacing inflation..

Liquidity Risk: is all about how easy it will be to turn your investment into cash when you want to. Some investments – like bonds – have liquidity built into them (at an agreed date in the future you will get paid your money back by the borrower) but not all do. This is where **Stock Exchanges** come in – allowing investors to trade with one another – getting their money into and out of investments. When we analyse investments we look at the **Liquidity** – i.e. how easy it is to trade. You would generally expect to pay more for (and get a lower return from) an investment that is **Highly Liquid** (remember – Cash is King because it is the most liquid investment out there). **Liquidity** can be very difficult to measure because when go through bad times liquidity can dry up – people tend to sit on their hands and there is less stock available to buy or sell. As a general rule though, shares and bonds issued by larger companies and Governments tend to be more liquid than those issued by smaller companies.

Rating Agencies (such as Moody's, S&P or Fitch) give bonds Credit Ratings that provide investors with a guide to how likely the company is to default. At one end of the scale are high quality Government or Sovereign Bonds from developed countries (like the UK or the USA). Corporate Bonds (those issued by companies) tend to rank lower down, they are divided into Investment Grade Bonds (from household names like Microsoft or Vodafone) and High Yield Bonds (from riskier smaller companies). The less likely an issuer is to default, the lower the rate of interest they will pay on their debt.

While Rating Agencies can provide a good guide that a lot of investors rely on, they were heavily criticised in the aftermath of the Financial Crisis for continuing to give good credit ratings to poor quality bonds.

Valuation Metrics

In order to compare different opportunities, investors use Valuation Metrics or Investor Ratios to help us compare apples with apples (as opposed to apples with spaceships).

We get the figures to fill out the ratios from the Financial Statements and Accounts that companies and governments must regularly release, and by making forecasts based on a range on our expectations of the future world. Much like weather forecasts, even highly educated guesses about the future are subject to error. I hate to pick on Michael Fish but:

"There is absolutely no chance of a hurricane hitting the UK."

It is impossible to cover all of the possible Valuation Metrics in this book. There are hundreds and people are inventing new ones all of the time so any definitive list would be out of date by the time I get this to print. Instead we're just going to focus on a few key ones that should help you understand the basic principles.

Yield: the income that we are paid from our investments is very important as it is often a large, more easily predictable part of your returns. To compare different investments with one another we talk about **Yield** – the percentage income return we are getting on our investment. It is calculated as;

YIELD = ANNUAL INCOME / PRICE OF BOND

If all other things are equal it would make more sense to go for an investment with a higher yield since it gives you a higher expected return.

Duration: is a way to measure how sensitive a **bond** is to changes in **Interest Rates** and is measured in **years**. Since we know that the value of bond investments goes up when interest rates go down and vice versa, it is important to know how much of an effect a move in rates will have.

There are quite a few ways to calculate duration (and it gets very mathematical) so I'm not going to go into all of that here. But the key is that a high figure means that a bond is more sensitive to moves in rates, while a low figure means a bond is less sensitive. Generally speaking bonds which pay higher rates of interest have a lower duration than those that pay less, and bonds with a shorter time to **maturity** (the date at which you get paid back) have a lower duration than those with a longer time left to run.

Earnings per Share (EPS): this ratio is primarily used by **Equity Investors. Earnings** is just another way of saying **Profits. Share Prices** on their own don't really tell you anything – they are just a number. A share that costs 1p is not necessarily cheaper than one that costs £1,000. It is more important to understand the share of **Earnings** that you are buying. **Market Capitalisation** (or Market Cap to its friends) is the total value of all the shares issued by a company so we calculate **EPS** like so.

EARNINGS PER SHARE = MARKET CAP / TOTAL No. OF SHARES

In isolation this still doesn't tell us all that much, but it is an important input for other calculations such as

Price / Earnings Ratio (P/E): this ratio helps us to understand how many years' worth of **earnings** we are paying up for in advance.

PRICE EARNINGS RATIO = SHARE PRICE / EARNINGS PER SHARE

This gives us a **multiple** which we can use to compare different companies. Let's look at the example below to see it in action.

	Company A	Company B
Share Price	100p	150p
Earnings per Share	10p	20p
Calculation	P/E = 100p / 10p	P/E = 150p / 20p
P/E Ratio:	**10x**	**7.5x**

So, here we can see that (despite having a higher share price) **Company B** is cheaper than **Company A**. When a company has a higher **P/E** it usually means that investors believe it will grow at a faster rate, or that the business is of a higher **quality** and will be more stable.

Net Asset Value (NAV): is a way to understand the underlying value of all of the **assets** a company owns, minus any **liabilities. Assets** can be anything from factories and machinery, to unsold stock in a warehouse. **Liabilities** are any debts or payments the company still needs to make.

NET ASSET VALUE = ASSETS – LIABILITIES

If you own your own house or flat you could do your own NAV calculation. Just take the current value of your property (based on what houses of a similar type are selling for on Rightmove or Zoopla) and take away the amount left to pay on your mortgage.

NAV can be useful for equity and bond investors – who might want to see if the company has any assets that it is not using and could sell if it gets into a tight spot. But it is also very useful for Property and Infrastructure investors looking to summarise the value of their investments.

I know that a lot of these ratios can be a bit hard to get your head around when they are given to you in a book. The best way I found to really understand them was to start using them. As a little exercise try taking two companies that operate in the same industry sector. Maybe consider Apple and Google, or Royal Dutch Shell and British Petroleum. Using freely available information online you should be able to put the ratios outlined above into a short table and compare the companies side by side. Think about why they might be valued differently and which you think might be better to buy if you could only pick one.

MILLENNIAL MONEY MANAGEMENT
Chapter 6 – Collective Investing

Hopefully, by now you're feeling much better equipped to tackle the world of investing. You've got your feet on firm Economic ground so you can understand how the world goes around. You know your **Major** and **Minor Asset Classes**. And you've got a basic idea of how to **analyse** investments and put them together to build a **Multi-Asset Portfolio**. But now we need to look at a practical way to get your savings invested, and I know that the problem for a lot of us is that we **lack the scale** to build a **well-diversified** portfolio.

Imagine it's getting to the end of a January. Christmas and New Year have dented your bank account and you got paid a bit early so you're scraping until payday. You've got to eat though, and you really fancy a good ol' fashioned Paella. A hearty, warming dish to banish the Winter blues.

So, you raid your change pot (the £2.48 you find is a bit of a let-down) and head out undeterred to the supermarket in search of ingredients.

It's January, and your New Year's resolution to cook more from scratch is so far intact, so the ready meal aisle is out of bounds. But, after consulting a certain TV chef's latest book and realising you forgot to grow your own herb garden, you're struggling to get all the ingredients you need to make a rounded, well-balanced meal.

Even the core ingredients come in quantities that are much too large for just you. The smallest 500g pack of rice is going to set you back £1, eating up a big portion of your budget. To make it work you can start cutting out ingredients, but the result is going to be an underwhelming dish of just-about flavoured rice – best consumed in a dark room while watching Oliver Twist to make yourself feel grateful for what you have.

Alternatively, maybe you could call up some of your friends who are in a similar situation. If a bunch of you all chip in your small sums, chances are you can get together most of the ingredients on Jamie's list. You can even share the costs and the effort of cooking the meal by eating together in one of your homes, all chipping a bit in to cover the gas bill and taking turns to stir the pot.

Now imagine your whole Facebook feed lights up with friends and family excited about your January Paella Extravaganza. Even your Mum's heard about it, although she promises she's not spying on you. With hundreds of you gathering for a huge feast you can afford all those little, fancy spice jars and a few glasses of Sangria for everyone to wash it down with. You can even afford to hire a professional chef and catering team to make the paella for you, since the cost will be spread amongst so many. You have successfully gone from a solitary bowl of gruel to a full-blown fiesta!

Collective Investments or Funds are a way for investors with smaller amounts of money to build well-diversified portfolios. When you buy a fund you are effectively pooling your money with other investors, allowing you to experience the benefits of scale. In particular you get access to **Fund Managers** who run the fund for you – buying and selling **underlying investments**.

Funds come in all shapes and sizes. Some of them are very generalist – and can contain all of the ingredients you need for a well-diversified multi-asset portfolio, while others can be incredibly specialised, focussing in on a specific niche in the market. Either you can buy into a full ready-made portfolio, or you can use them as building blocks and carry out your own **asset allocation**.

Funds tend to fall in to three main categories: **Open-Ended Investment Companies (OEICs), Investment Trusts (ITs) and Exchange Traded Funds (ETFs)**.

Open-ended Investment Companies (OEICs): are also known as **Unit Trusts** (or **Mutual Funds** in the USA). The **Fund Managers** make investments in line with the fund's objectives, and each day the **Fund Administrators** calculate the **Net Asset Value** of the fund. Investors can buy or sell units in the fund through the Fund Administrators (usually once a day).

The fund grows and shrinks in size depending on the number of investors who buy and sell units. If the fund grows because it experiences **inflows**, then the **Fund Managers** will invest the additional money in line with their strategy. However, if the fund shrinks because it experiences **outflows**, they will sell some of the underlying holdings to meet the requests for capital (or **redemptions**).

Investment Trusts (ITs): are also known as **Closed-Ended Funds**. These are listed on a **Stock Exhange** and are traded between investors in the same way as **Equities**. They are effectively run like a listed company, but the assets of the company are investments. Unlike in an **OEIC** investors can get their money in and out more regularly. Shares in Investment Trusts are bought and sold on stock exchanges in the same way as equities.

The Investment Trust is limited in size to the number of shares it has in issue and the value of them – it's **Market Capitalisation**. This means that if the **demand** for shares outstrips **supply** the shares of the Investment Trust can trade at a **Premium** to **NAV** (i.e. you will pay more for the shares than the value of the underlying investments). Conversely, if demand for the shares fall it is possible to buy shares at a **Discount** to **NAV**.

The **Fund Managers** are free to just worry about investing the money, they do not have to consider how many investors might put money into the fund or take it out each day. This can allow them the freedom to invest in less **liquid** investments (since they won't need to sell them just to meet **outflows**). However, the **Premium** and **Discount** bring in an additional element of risk – the value of your holding can go up or down based on shifts in supply and demand, as well as due to the performance of the underlying investments. In an **OEIC** you will buy and sell at **NAV**.

Exchange-Traded Funds (ETFs): are a bit of a hybrid of the **OEICs** and **ITs**. They are **open-ended** in that the Fund Administrators create or cancel units based on demand. But (as suggested by the name) they are listed and traded on stock exchanges, throughout the day like **Investment Trusts**.

ETFs are most commonly used for **passive investment strategies** which we're going to look at next.

Benchmarks: are used by investors to measure the overall performance of certain markets. They are also known as **Indexes**. You will probably have heard some of their names already – the FTSE 100 is a benchmark made up of the 100 largest companies in the UK, while the S&P 500 represents the largest 500 US companies. Fund Managers are required to provide investors with a fair benchmark to measure them against that is representative of their investment strategy. They are usually built using a methodology based on **Market Capitalisation** – the bigger a company is, the more of the Index it represents.

Passive and Active Investment

When we go about picking a **Fund Manager** we need to first think about whether we want our money **Passively** or **Actively Managed**. There are advantages and disadvantages to either strategy, and your overall portfolio might contain some of each.

Passively Managed funds aim to track a certain **Index**. Passive investors argue the markets are **highly efficient** – it is hard for an investor to be cleverer than average, and markets will naturally find the right price (or fair value) for each investment. Therefore, they argue that it makes more sense to replicate the shares in the market. In this scenario the **Fund Manager** is like a security guard watching CCTV – keeping an eye on things, but not really going out of his or her way to investigate.

They buy and sell investments in order to meet inflows and outflows if necessary, but otherwise just follow what the index is doing. When new shares enter or exit the index the managers **rebalance** the portfolio accordingly.

Actively Managed funds attempt to generate returns that are higher than the Index by buying a smaller sub-set of investments that the managers hope will **outperform** the index. The Fund Managers are more like private detectives, analysing companies and seeking out the best possible investment opportunities.

Active Fund Managers argue that markets are **inefficient**. They don't always get things right and therefore, with enough research and the right strategy it is possible to generate a higher return. Fund Managers will often talk about their **Process**; the way in which they find the companies they believe will outperform and how they build their portfolios.

There is also the possibility that the Fund Managers may not actually outperform the market, so you could end up paying more in fees for a lower return.

Active	VS	Passive
Active managers give you the chance to **outperform** the market, since the fund manager is making decisions on what to invest in. However, there is the risk they can **underperform** as well	Returns	The fund will only ever deliver a return in line with the market minus fees and expenses
As the investment process is usually far more intensive and requires more human involvement, active funds are generally more expensive than passive ones	Costs	Since the investment process is less resource intensive, passive funds tend to be much lower cost. Through certain passive funds it is possible to get access to markets for as low as 0.07% p.a. and some providers are even experimenting with free index tracking funds
While active funds will give investors a guide to their intended strategy, it is possible that the fund manager may start to move away from it over time. This is known as **Style Drift**	Strategy	IPassive funds have a clear investment strategy that is outlined before you invest. Since this is often automated it is much less likely that you will experience **Style Drift** in a passive fund
If the Fund Manager believes we are entering a downturn, they can take action to change the portfolio accordingly. They can react to the world around them and try to protect their investors money.	Defensive Measures	Passive fund managers are usually prevented from taking defensive action by their rules. Regardless of what happens in the wider world the fund will continue to hold its investments

Investment Style

Active investors usually describe themselves as having a certain **Style**. This indicates the types of stocks and bonds that they believe will outperform the wider market.

In equity investment in particular there are two major schools of thought: **Growth** and **Value**.

Growth Investors: prefer to focus on **high quality** companies that can consistently grow their **earnings** faster than the market.

Growth investors tend to be comfortable paying a higher price for their investments, believing that if a company's earnings grow quickly an expensive starting valuation can look a lot more appealing with time. One of the world's most famous investors Warren Buffet believes that if you pick a really good company you should never really have to trade, you should just hold on to it.

Fund managers who follow this style tend to look for companies with high **barriers to entry**. The last thing they want is for another company to swoop in and start stealing market share from their investment. Factors such as branding play a big role, as do things like distribution networks – as an example, it would be quite hard for us to go out and start a company that competes directly with Amazon. Amazon have an incredibly strong brand and have built out a distribution network that allowed me to order a new keyboard towards the end of Chapter 4 that arrived before the end of Chapter 5! Investors sometimes refer to factors such as these as **moats**.

Value Investors: place a lot of focus on **valuation**. They believe that, with a huge list of potential investments to choose from, they should focus on buying companies at cheap prices. When companies go through a bit of a rough patch; maybe a change in management or a fall in earnings due to a one-off issue, a lot of investors avoid them. As a result the share prices can become unfairly low.

This is where value investors like to swoop in. They believe that, as long as the company is only suffering short-term problems rather than long-term decline – the share prices should recover to more normal levels and they will be able to sell at a profit.

Dividends also provide a degree of support for value investors. If there is nothing wrong with the overall business model then the company should be able to continue paying investors. This is sometimes called being **paid to wait**.

Of course, value investors have to be careful that they don't walk in to **value traps**. An investment can appear very cheap based on current prices , but if the business is in decline it could become even cheaper. If investing with a value style it helps to be particularly aware of potential **Disruptors**. **Disruptors** come along and shake up existing markets, usually with new technology or a different business model. We live in an age of disruption; AirBnB for instance is disrupting the global hotel industry, while Uber is disrupting the taxi market.

Analysing Funds

When it comes to analysing potential fund investments there are another huge series of **Investor Ratios** and metrics that investors use, the following are just a few of the key ones to get you going.

Beta: is a measure of risk relative to the wider market that the fund is investing in. A Beta of 1 means that the fund is exactly as risky as the market – we would expect an ETF tracking a certain index to have a Beta of close to or exactly 1. Meanwhile, a Beta of 0.5 means the fund is half as risky as the market – if the market fell by 10% we would expect the fund to fall by 5%, but similarly if the market rose by 10% we would only expect the fund to rise by 5%.

Alpha: is the primary way in which we measure **active managers**. Once we have accounted for the **market return** (using **Beta**) anything above this is excess return or **Alpha**. Assuming the fund has a Beta of 1 (it is taking exactly the same risk as the market), and the market generates a return of 10% over the year. If the fund generates a return of 12%, we would say the **Alpha** is 2%. It is possible for Alpha to be a negative figure; this indicates the Fund Managers are not doing a very good job! We should also expect Fund Managers to generate Alpha that at the very least pays for their fees.

Volatility: is another way of measuring risk and can be applied to funds as well as individual investments. It is a statistical measure used to explain how much prices vary over a certain period. It would be possible to write an entire PhD thesis on volatility (several Finance Professors have). However, the key thing to remember is that a higher volatility score will likely mean a bumpier ride. Assuming you use the same source for your volatility figure you can compare funds with one another and the wider market, giving you an idea of whether you're about to get on a Tea Cup Ride at the village fete or Nemesis at Alton Towers.

Tracking Error: is a measure of how much a funds returns differ from those of the index. It is useful to check whether **Passive Funds** are keeping track of the index well, and if **Active Managers** are building a varied enough portfolio to potentially beat it. One thing to watch out for is **closet trackers**. These are funds that charge active fees for management but are playing it safe and hugging the index. If your manager is not diverging from the index then you would be better off in a cheaper, passive fund.

Using funds it is possible to make good portfolios with even small amounts of money. This solves one of the biggest problems when it comes to investing; having enough cash to start without taking an unacceptable level of risk. Fund providers are very good at making information about their funds available to everybody (it is how they make money after all). When you are starting out take advantage of this and read / watch / listen to whatever you can get your hands on. Use the lessons we've covered in this chapter to pick apart what the fund managers are telling you. But always remember one thing:

If it sounds too good to be true.....it probably is.

How financial services companies market their products to investors is a focus of regulators (like the FCA in the UK). However, there are regularly firms who will push the boundaries. Always remember that **Returns** don't come without **Risks**. I would always advise you to be very cautious if anyone tells you they have found a way to generate returns without taking risks.

MILLENNIAL MONEY MANAGEMENT

Chapter 7 – Financial Planning

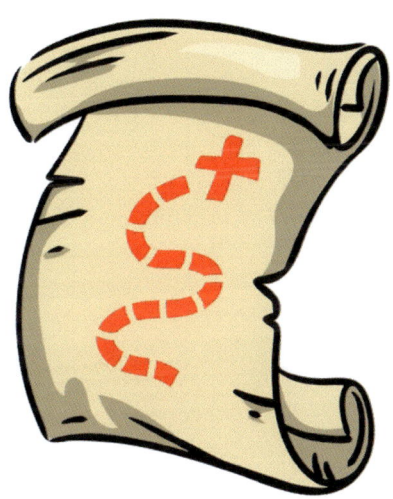

Life is a big journey, so when we're thinking about investing for the future it helps to make yourself a map. You shouldn't be in a rush to navigate to the end, but it helps to know what direction you're heading in, what goals you have and what obstacles you might face along the way.

It's important to be aware of your own limits. While my DIY course gave me the confidence to put up some shelves around the house and mount my own TV to the wall (it hasn't fallen down yet), I'm not messing around with the electrics. There are times when it is best to consult a professional who can help you, and when it comes to **Financial Planning**, I would always consider seeking out a Financial Planner or **Financial Advisor** to give you a hand.

By knowing what you are trying to achieve it is possible to get better value out of the process; if you can do some of the legwork and be better prepared ahead of meeting with your advisor, you can save time and potentially money. You can also avoid getting taken advantage of. I've met a huge amount of great Financial Planners during my career, but as in every trade there are a few bad apples out there and knowing what to expect from the process can be really helpful.

The key steps to financial planning are:

1. Determine your current financial position. The first step is to work out exactly where you are now. It's worth starting with a very basic spreadsheet, that summarises the value of your **assets** (cash in the bank, investments, equity in your home etc) in one column and your **liabilities** in the other (your outstanding mortgage, and details of any other loans or debts you have).

Assets		Liabilities	
Current Account Balance	£2500	Mortgage Debt	£112,000
Cash Savings Account	£12,000	Student Loan	£1460
Stocks & Shares ISA	£27,500	Car Loan	£3600
Pension	£22,400		
Equity in Home	£78,000		

It will also help if you can have a clear idea of your **income** and **spending patterns**. How much do you have coming in and going out a month? Are you likely to receive a bonus?

2. Developing Financial Goals. Financial Goals can be pretty much anything you want them to be, and there are no right or wrong answers. Perhaps you want to start putting aside money to send your kids to University or want to move into that house on your street that you've always loved. Maybe you dream of spending your retirement climbing the world's biggest mountains.

Understanding what your financial goals are will help you and your advisor to work out what you are trying to achieve.

3. Identify and Consider Alternatives. Your advisor can help you go through alternatives to the current action you are taking. There are things you may not have considered that a second pair of eyes will pick-up. For example, if you have any outstanding debts it might be more sensible to pay these off before you consider investing your surplus cash.

4. Create and Implement a Financial Plan. Based on all of the information that you have gathered together your advisor will help you put together a Financial Plan. They will help you decide how much of your wealth to place in different accounts and investments, and will offer you advice on how to make sure you are being **tax-efficient**.

Tax-efficiency (sensible) and **Tax-evasion** (illegal) sound similar but they are very different things. Tax-evasion is where people purposefully avoid paying the tax that they owe – hiding investments from their local authorities or taking cash payments and not declaring them. **Tax-efficiency** is where you use approved schemes to reduce your overall tax bill. Pensions are a great example of this – the Government want us to save for our own retirement, so they have created tax incentives to encourage us to do so. In the UK and many other countries, savings you make into your pension will go out of your pay cheque before any tax is taken away.

5. Give your plan a regular check-up. Your financial plan is not something you should make once and never question again. You want to come back to it regularly and confirm that it is still the right one. Things change in our lives and we should be ready to change our plans accordingly.

Much like your Dentist, you're going to want to meet your Financial Planner regularly (hopefully it will be a more enjoyable experience). You should also reconsider your plan and speak with your advisor if you experience any **major life events**, such as getting a new job, or finding out you're about to become a parent.

Robo-Advisors: first appeared in 2008, but really started to gain traction from 2010. They are essentially AI programmes designed to help cut the costs of getting investment advice.

Robo-advice is still in its infancy but can be a useful tool to consider; a lot of companies provide **risk profiling** services to help you understand what investment strategies might be right for you. They also benefit from being far cheaper than human-led financial planning.

Of course, there are limitations. We are still a long way off fully intelligent AI, and in most cases the software they use is limited by the inputs you provide – putting more pressure on you to get the information you provide right. My Alexa is a fine example of this. I'm beginning to think she doesn't like my taste in music and is just choosing her own instead.

Financial planning is a key component to having a healthy financial future. Good planning will help you to focus on what is important and save a lot of sleepless nights. It is something a lot of us put off as too big a task, but the earlier you start the easier the task will be.

Talking about Death

Most people are afraid of dying (it's a rational fear in my opinion), and as a result don't like to talk about it. But it's something we need to get a bit better at.

A lot of us aren't just thinking about ourselves when we consider our finances, we're thinking about the people we love. The most important thing you can do, if you haven't done it already, is to make a **will** and keep it up to date. When people pass away without leaving a will, it can cause months and years of delays dividing their assets. It can even cause families to fall out at a point where they are all vulnerable. Wills are where you can set out exactly what you want to happen when you die, both financially (who you want to leave money to) and non-financially (maybe you'd like your body to be shot in to space on one of Elon Musk's rockets). Regardless of how young you are it is a good idea to make sure you have a will. Review it regularly and make sure it stays up to date with changes in your life.

There are several other things about death that we might need to consider. Some people may have to think about **Inheritance Tax**. Others might want to make sure some of their money is left for a family member who might not be able to look after it themselves and need to form a **Trust**. As a general rule if these are things you need to think about it makes sense to deal with them with a Financial Advisor. You may not like the idea of paying the fees, but the more complex your needs become the more money you will save in the long run by doing things right first time.

Chapter 8 – Investing for Impact

Hopefully by now you are convinced of the financial impact of investing, but finally I think it's worth talking about the non-financial impact it can have. At their core financial markets are a transfer mechanism. Investors come to the market to place their money with people who can earn them a return, while Companies come to the market seeking money with which to fuel their growth.

But you don't just have to go along for the ride and give your money to anyone who wants it, and as an investor can use your influence to change the way in which business is conducted around the world.

Screening

You can choose not to invest in companies operating in certain industries; for example, you might not want to own Tobacco companies because you don't want to support smoking. Or perhaps you don't want to invest in any companies that operate in parts of the world where human-rights are not respected. This is called **Negative Screening**.

Alternatively, you can choose to reward the behaviours and impacts on society that you believe are good. For instance, you might invest in companies that have strong workplace wellbeing policies in place. This is known as **Positive Screening**.

Regardless of how you decide what is and isn't included in your portfolio, you will have an impact on the market. If certain companies have fewer buyers because of the impact their business is having will not be able to achieve as strong **valuations**. This in turn will affect how easy it is for entrepreneurs starting businesses in certain sectors to raise money. Thinking back to our farmer; if there is little demand for chocolate but a high demand for coffee, she is more likely to plant coffee.

There are a lot of grey areas within this area of investing, and I don't have any desire to tell you what to believe. Some of you might want to exclude a company like Apple from their portfolio because of how they treat their workforce in China, while others might want to include it because of the benefits health and fitness apps have brought to people. Some might want to include only car companies that are pushing to develop electric vehicles, while others may exclude them because of the environmental damage of digging for the rare earth metals needed to make the batteries. The key thing is that it is up to you, and you have the option to express your views and make a difference if you want to.

Another way you can get your opinions across is through **Shareholder Activism** (don't worry, you don't have to make a sign). However, as an equity owner you do have the right to **vote** on certain issues. Companies hold an **Annual General Meeting** or **AGM** once a year (and if there is an emergency will hold an **Extraordinary General Meeting** or **EGM**). This allows company management (who effectively work for the shareholders) to consult the company's owners about the course they should set. Shareholders will be invited to vote on a range of issues;

from the pay of top management, to whether or not to proceed with taking over another company. Shareholders also vote to appoint board members to their positions.

Greenwashing; is something you have to be on the lookout for if certain issues matter to you. Well run companies tend to employ very good salespeople, and sometimes managers can be the best of all. Generally, managers tend to put a positive spin on their business, and with the high level of publicity currently being directed at environmental concerns there is a tendency to exaggerate the positive impacts companies make. Always take what management say with a hefty pinch of salt, and don't just rely on their reports for your information.

Health Warning!!! While investing for impact might sound good to you it is worth being aware of the risks. An **Investment Universe** is all the possible investments that you might consider, research and select to build your portfolio. The moment you start screening out certain companies based on the industries they operate in, or the way they conduct business you are shrinking the size of your Universe.

For example, if you decide that you don't want to invest in any companies that drill for oil then (regardless of how good value they look) you won't consider them and there's no way they would enter your portfolio. If the price of oil then skyrockets (and the share prices of those companies follows) you will miss out. At certain times it may be impossible to keep up with the performance of your wider benchmark if you exclude certain companies and industries.

Investing through funds

Ethical or Socially Responsible Investing (SRI) has been gaining an increasing amount of traction within the investment community, and as such an increasing amount of fund managers are launching funds that cater to the growing demand.

As such, there are an increasing amount of options available to investors who would like to align their investments with their personal views. The downside when investing in funds is that it is harder to translate your exact views into the eventual portfolio. For instance, you might not like smoking and want to exclude tobacco companies but think that there is nothing wrong with alcohol. But, it is easier to find funds that exclude a wide range of so called **Sin Stocks** (Alcohol, Tobacco, Weapons, Gambling etc) than it is to find funds that exclude specific sectors. The fund managers are aiming to cater to a wide range of views, to please as many of their investors as possible.

Fund Managers are required to be very specific about how they will invest your money, and as such they produce a wide variety of documents and video interviews talking about their funds. These are the best resource for understanding what they will and won't invest in. You can also usually see a list of their biggest investments (and in some cases every share held within the fund) – but don't rely entirely upon this. A fund might not hold any companies in a certain sector right now, but this may be because the Fund Manager doesn't see them as a good investment – if the share prices fell tomorrow they might look to include them after all.

MILLENNIAL MONEY MANAGEMENT
Conclusion

Our time together is coming to an end. Of course, this was far from a comprehensive guide and there are volumes that we skipped over or simply did not have the time or space to cover at all. But I hope that this book was enough to get you excited. Thinking about your financial future can be daunting, but by reaching this point you have taken the first steps and I hope you carry on from here.

One of the best things about a subject as big as Finance is that there is always room to keep on learning. I thought to round out this book it would be great to share three lessons that I have picked up during my time in the industry. Again, these are far from comprehensive, but they are the ones that always stick in my brain when I am thinking about investing.

1. The Taxi Driver Principle

I once had dinner with a Fund Manager from New York, and one thing he said has stuck in my mind ever since. Her life involved an awful lot of air miles as she flew between NYC, London, Beijing and everywhere in between to meet with companies and investors. But along with the flights came the taxi rides at the other end.

Assuming you don't keep your headphones on, and your music turned up most taxi drivers will be keen to have a good chat with you during your ride. If you mention you work in finance the conversation often turns to investment ideas!

A lot of active investment involves seeing things differently to other people. To beat the average return of the market you need to see something that other people don't. So be extra careful when everybody you talk to is extremely positive or negative on a certain idea. If everybody is talking about the next great investment (including your friendly taxi driver) then the chances are that the good news is already reflected in the price. Pay remarkably close attention to valuation when you are considering an idea that everybody else supports. Try to play devil's advocate and ask what they could have all missed. Even if you can't find anything the process will make you a better investor.

2. It's not Monopoly Money

This one came from my very first mentor, on my very first day of work in the industry. There is a danger when you are dealing with relatively large amounts of money that you can forget that it is all very real. Once the zeros start adding up you can become detached from reality as it becomes harder and harder to imagine holding that money in your hands.

My boss was keen to impart on his young recruit that all the money we managed belonged to someone. Maybe it had taken them a long time to earn. Perhaps it was a gift from a family member who had skimped and saved so that they could have it. He wanted me to understand that it was a privilege to look after it for them and to not get lost in the numbers on the screen. This is still a lesson I take the time to teach every trainee I have ever been responsible for.

For some of you this book might be the first step towards a financial career, while for others it might just be your own savings that you are thinking about. Regardless, this is a lesson I want you to take away with you. When you consider making investments and taking risks take the time to think about what it took to make the money in the first place. Don't ever forget that it took time to earn. Remember that the savings in your account represent holidays you didn't go on and nice things that you didn't buy.

3. Don't marry your ideas

I'm getting married next year so this one particularly resonates with me! Unlike in your personal life, the world of investment does not reward love and loyalty. Don't get too attached to any of your investment ideas.

When we manage other people's money it is required that we write clear notes to document our rationale. We must explain why we bought or sold investments in order to create a paper trail that anyone could pick up and understand. This is particularly important so that we can prove we were not acting recklessly if something goes wrong. However, I find it incredibly useful outside of this purpose. It is important to challenge yourself about your ideas. I like to regularly go back and look at my notes to see exactly why I thought it was a good idea to buy something.

We all make mistakes when investing. It simply comes with the territory of trying to predict the future. But one thing to be particularly careful of is changing your rationale to suit a new set of circumstances. Investors can become wedded to their ideas and refuse to let them go even though things have changed. Sometimes it makes sense to hold on to an investment that hasn't performed well. For instance, a company you bought into might have just gone through a bad patch but your underlying reasons for buying the shares could remain the same.

I find it useful to ask myself if I would be comfortable buying more and increasing the size of my position. If the answer is no, then I ask myself why I am still holding on. And if my investment rationale has changed due to the new circumstances then I force myself to start over and write out a new research note based on the new facts.

I'm not suggesting that you should start writing comprehensive investment research. However, I recommend that you take the time when making an investment to put down a few lines about why you think it is a good idea. This way when it comes time to make a regular review of your investments you will have something to refer to and challenge yourself with. Never forget that it is better to walk away from an idea that no longer makes sense. Holding on when you lack a reason to is always a gamble.

Finally, thank you for taking the time to read this book. It was a lot of fun to write and if it has helped you in even a small way then I consider it time very well spent. One of the problems I have had with investment over my entire career is how shut off it is from the real world. I worry that like many other professions (I'm looking at you lawyers!) we have closed it off from the wider public. We have wrapped investing up in complicated language, daunting numbers and made ourselves the gatekeepers of this knowledge. I hope that by writing this book I am helping to unlock that gate and throw away the key.

Thank You!

To my Fiancée Alyona, without whose constant support (and a little loving nagging) this project would never have made it to the end. She has always been my artistic inspiration, guide, and my best friend.

To my mentors Bill, Brian, Nicky, Robin and Scott whose collective knowledge I have ransacked to put this book together.

To Artem for his amazing illustrations that have really helped to liven up a somewhat dry subject. Please check out more of his work at www.behance.net/ikmanufactory.

To Matt and Jens for their help in proof-reading, grammar-checking and common-sense injecting!

To Olga for the fantastic work on editing and publishing, taking the jumble off my computer and turning it into the book you have in your hands. You can find more of her work at https://cargocollective.com/OlgaRudenko.

MILLENNIAL MONEY MANAGEMENT
Glossary

Active Management: a type of fund management where the managers try to be different to the index in order to beat it.

Advice Gap: a term coined to describe the increasing number of people who lack access to financial advice.

Analyst: a specific job role focussed on research.

Asset Classes: groups of investments that have similar features and risks to one another.

Bears: economists and investors who believe the economy is going to contract from its current point.

Benchmarks: a collection of investments used as a yardstick to compare your own or your fund manager's performance against.

Bonds: instruments issued by companies and governments to represent a debt that they owe.

Boom: a term used to describe a particularly long or large economic expansion.

Bulls: economists and investors who believe the economy is going to expand from its current point.

Cash: not necessarily just paper money, but also money held in an accessible bank account.

Circular Flow Model: a key economic model that explains how goods, services, labour and payments are transferred between Households, Firms and Governments.

Command Economies / Planned Economies: where the government controls all aspects of the economy – deciding what gets produced and how it is distributed amongst the people.

Compounding Returns: when returns from investment start to build over multiple years you effectively start getting paid "interest on interest". By reinvesting returns from previous years returns can start to grow exponentially.

Costs: the fees and charges associated with managing money that are charged to fund investors.

Coupon: the interest payment made to a bondholder.

Cycle / Economic Cycle: a way economists describe how the economy moves between periods of expansion and recession.

Default: when a company or government cannot pay its debts to lenders or suppliers and collapses.

Demand: the level of desire from consumers and households to purchase a specific good or service.

Depression: a term used to describe a particularly long or large recession.

Discretionary Management: where someone has the right to make investment decisions without consulting you first. Fund managers tend to have discretion as long as they stick to their agreed strategy.

Diversification: the process of splitting up your investments so that you are not overly exposed to any one key driver of risk or return.

Dividends: payments made by companies to shareholders.

Equilibrium: the price at which supply and demand meet and are balanced.

Equities: instruments issued by companies representing ownership.

Expansion: a period of economic growth.

Financial Planning: thinking about your current position and your future needs, and what you need to do to achieve them.

Firms: another term for companies (used by economists). They produce goods and services to sell to Households and Governments for a profit.

Funds: also known as Collective Investments, are a way for investors to pool their money together and benefit from scale and expertise.

Fiscal Policy: the way in which governments allocate their spending to exert some control over the economy.

Free Market Economies: where the government takes a back seat and politicians allow markets for labour, goods and services to balance themselves.

Fund Manager / Portfolio Manager: a specific job role focussed on managing a portfolio of investments on other people's behalf.

Government: a group of people who hold the authority to govern a country or state.

Households: groups of regular people like us who form groups to live in.

Indicators: different factors used by economists to understand where an economy is and where it is likely to go. They can be backwards looking (Lagging Indicators) or forwards looking (Leading Indicators).

Inflation: an economic measure of how much the prices of goods and services increase over time.

Interest: the income paid to a lender or cash depositor.

Investment Universe: all of the possible investments you might consider for your portfolio.

Investor Ratios: equations used by investors to work out the valuation of a particular investment and compare it with other similar alternatives.

Labour: a hard day's work (or any type of work for that matter).

Liquidity: a measure of how easy it is to buy or sell an investment – things can either be liquid (easy to trade) or illiquid (infrequently traded).

Markets: any place where two parties (a buyer and a seller) come together to exchange goods.

Mixed Economies: those that combine elements of Free Market Economies and Command Economies to land somewhere in the middle.

Monetary Policy: the way in which Central Banks exert control over an economy by increasing and decreasing the supply of money.

Opportunity Cost: the idea that time a decision is made to do something you have also decided not to do other things which could have had value.

Passive Management: a type of fund management where the managers try to replicate a certain index.

Peak: a high point of economic expansion.

Portfolio: a collection of assets combined so that the owner can benefit from diversification.

Prices: the value at which a specific good or service changes hands. Influenced by Supply and Demand.

Purchasing Power: the value of money based on the goods and services it will actually buy you at a given time.

Recession: a period of economic contraction or slow down.

Resources: can either refer to something physical (e.g. steel) or less tangible (e.g. labour).

Return: the money we receive back from investments. It includes any change in the value of the investment while it is held and any cashflows (such as dividends or interest) received.

Risk: the potential to lose money when investing in an asset. Risk takes on a number of different forms but ultimately comes down to the possibility that the value of your investments could go down.

Scarcity: an economic assumption that all resources are finite, forcing us to decide how best to use them.

Screening: the act of excluding certain investments from your portfolio based on easily identifiable characteristics or features.

Shortage: when demand outweighs supply – usually drives prices higher.

Supply: the amount of a specific good or service that is available to purchase.

Surplus: when supply outweighs demand – usually drives prices lower.

Taxes: the way in which Governments raise money from Households and Firms in order to fund the services it provides for its people.

Trough: the low point of an economic contraction.

Valuation: the way in which investors determine whether an investment is cheap or expensive.

Printed in Great Britain
by Amazon

54625281R00043